❦ History *of* Britain ❦

Victorian Children

Jane Shuter

Illustrated by James Field

HAMLYN

HISTORY OF BRITAIN – VICTORIAN CHILDREN
was produced for Hamlyn Children's Books
by Lionheart Books, London

Editor: Lionel Bender
Designer: Ben White
Editorial Assistant: Madeleine Samuel
Picture Researcher: Jennie Karrach
Media Conversion and Typesetting:
 Peter MacDonald

Educational Consultant: Sarah Levitt MA, AMA
Editorial Advisors: Andrew Farrow, Paul Shuter

Production Controller: Christine Campbell
Editorial Director: David Riley

First published in Great Britain in 1995
by Hamlyn Children's Books,
an imprint of Reed Children's Books,
Michelin House, 81 Fulham Road, London SW3 6RB,
and Auckland, Melbourne, Singapore and Toronto.

Copyright © 1995 Reed International Books Limited

ISBN 0 600 58605 7 Hb
ISBN 0 600 58606 5 Pb

British Library Cataloguing-in-Publication Data.
A catalogue record for this book is available
from the British Library.

Printed in Italy

Acknowledgements
All artwork by James Field.
Map on page 23 by Hayward Art Group.

Photo credits
The Mansell Collection: pages 4 (left), 5 (top left), 13 (top right),
15 (bottom right), 16 (left). Hulton Deutsch Collection: pages 6
(bottom left), 9 (top), 10 (bottom left), 11, 12 (top), 16 (right), 17
(top, bottom), 19 (centre), 22 (top). Fine Art Photographic
Library: pages 5 (top right), 6 (right), 7 (top right), 15 (centre),
21 (bottom). Robert Opie Collection: pages 4 (right), 7 (bottom),
8 (bottom left), 10 (top, bottom right), 14 (top), 14-15, 16 (bottom), 18 (top, bottom), 19 (bottom), 20 (bottom), 21 (centre),
with Gunnersbury Park Museum, London. Birmingham City
Council: page 7 (top left). The Salvation Army Heritage Centre:
pages 8 (bottom right), 15 (top), 22 (bottom right). Mary Evans
Picture Library: pages 8 (top), 12 (bottom). Bridgeman Art
Library: pages 7 (bottom: from Newcastle University), 13 (top
left: from Birmingham City Museums and Art Gallery), 13 (centre:
from Royal Holloway and Bedford New College, Surrey), 13 (bottom: from Guildhall Library, Corporation of London). e.t. archive:
page 21 (top: from Russell Coates Art Gallery). ZEFA: page 22
(bottom left).

Cover: Main illustration by John James, icons by Jonathan Adams.
Photo credits: Rattle, Book cover, Sports book - Robert Opie
Collection. Governor and children - Hulton Deutsch Collection.

PLACES TO VISIT

Here are some museums and houses which contain exhibits about
Victorian children. Your local tourist office will be able to tell you
about places to visit in your area.

The Argory, Dungannon, County Tyrone, Ireland. A collection of
Victorian rooms and furniture.
Bethnal Green Museum of Childhood, London. A huge collection
of toys, puppets and clothes.
Buckingham Palace, London. Many statues, objects and furniture
from Victorian times.
Castle Museum, York. Houses a reconstructed Victorian street, with
shops full of fascinating objects.
Cragside, Rothbury, Northumberland. A Victorian mansion; first
house to be lit by hydroelectricity.
Dickens House, Doughty St, London. Concentrates on the life of
Charles Dickens, but also gives general Victorian flavour.
Gunnersbury Park Museum, London. Victorian kitchens, just
restored. Other 'themed' exhibitions of trades and activities
through the ages, including laundry work! Costume collection.
Highland Folk Museum, Kingussie, Scotland. Traditional homes
recreated. It also has a farming museum.
Hughenden Manor, near High Wycombe, Bucks. Home of Prime
Minister Benjamin Disraeli, who lived there until his death in 1881.
Linley Sambourne House, Stafford Terrace, Kensington, London.
A late Victorian town house. Furniture, decorations and everyday
objects.
Museum of Childhood, Edinburgh, Scotland. A vast collection of
toys, puzzles and books. Displays of costume and on chimney
sweeps.
Museum of Childhood, Beaumaris, Gwynedd. Small museum,
crammed full of toys, musical boxes, magic lanterns, clockwork
figures and money boxes.
Museum of English Rural Life, Reading. Farming tools, smocks,
machinery (including steam) and recreated farmhouse rooms.
National Trust Museum of Childhood, Sudbury Hall, Sudbury,
Derbyshire. Toys and displays. Has a chimney climb for the
adventurous!
North of England Open Air Museum, Beamish, County Durham.
Themed areas connected by trams or buses, including a colliery
with miners' cottages, a farm and a Victorian schoolroom.
Osborne House, Isle of Wight. Queen Victoria's seaside home, built
at her own expense in 1845. Her private rooms have been
preserved unaltered.
Preston Manor, Preston Park, Brighton, Sussex. Lots of everyday
Victorian furniture and objects.
Quarry Bank Mill, Styal, Cheshire. Water-powered, working cotton
industry museum. Apprentice house shows life in the 1830s.
Shugborough Estate, near Stafford, Staffs. Being restored as a
19th-century working estate. House has recreated kitchens,
laundry and brew-house.
Standen House, East Grinstead, W. Sussex. Dates from 1890; filled
with furniture, pottery and pictures as well as everyday objects.
Original electric lights.
Tintagel Old Post Office, Tintagel, Cornwall. A restored Victorian
letter-receiving office.
V&A Museum, London. The building is an excellent example of
architecture of the time. Inside you can find examples of clothes
and everyday objects.
Welsh Folk Museum, St. Fagans, Cardiff. Recreated rooms and
houses; displays on farming and mining. Victorian farm, chapel
and school can be seen in use.

INTRODUCTION

What was life like for children in England in the reign of Queen Victoria (1837-1901)? Everything depended on how rich their parents were. The rich, upper classes owned most of the land and had most of the power. The government did not believe in 'interfering' with the way that people lived, even to help them. So they did little to help the many people who were trying to live on less than £1 a week, just enough to pay the rent and buy bread, potatoes and coal.

New inventions changed everyday life. Many people still lived and worked in the country. But towns grew fast, especially where factories were set up and homes were built for the workers. Railways spread all over the country. People could travel more easily and cheaply.

CONTENTS

RICH AND POOR

"They are like two nations that have no contact or sympathy. They know as little of each other's habits, thoughts and feelings as if they lived on different planets," wrote Benjamin Disraeli in 1846. He was talking about the rich and poor of Victorian Britain.

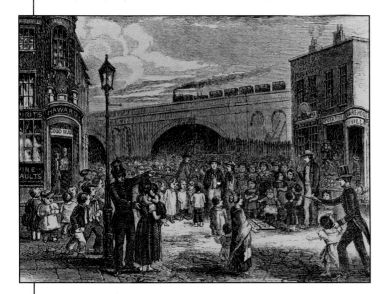

▷ **A London street in about 1865.** The carts, omnibuses and cabs are pulled by horses. Boys sweep muck from the cobbles. Regular horse-drawn bus services had begun in the 1830s.

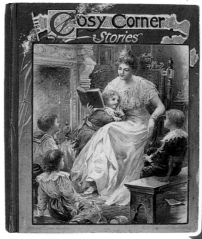

△ **A hiring fair at Spitalfields, London, in 1850.** Poor children came here to hire themselves out to work as temporary servants.

▷ **Children of wealthy parents did not have to find work.** They were well looked after. They stayed at home, playing or reading books like this one.

Disraeli, an MP in 1846 and Prime Minister later, was right. Rich people lived on large country estates and also had big houses in fashionable towns like London or Bath. They had servants to do everything for them, even bring up the children. Rich children had lots of toys and clothes and were well fed, but they were brought up very strictly. A saying from the time, "children should be seen and not heard", meant they had to be quiet, obedient and always neat. Boys were sent away to private schools from the age of seven. Girls stayed at home to learn to be a rich man's wife. Children of middle-class people like doctors and lawyers lived in comfortable homes and were well dressed and fed. They had fewer toys, but strict rules too.

△ **A flower seller** at work in London.

◁ **Poor people lived in terrible slums**, as this cartoon from 1852 shows.

◁ **Rich and poor people pass each other on the street.** The poor are working, selling flowers, driving carts and cabs, and sweeping the street. The rich are shopping or travelling across the city.

To the rich, towns like London were places to have fun – to go to theatres, dances and parties, and to spend their money. To the poor they were places where they might, if they were lucky, find work. Poor children had to work too, as soon as they could, often from the age of six upwards. They lived in the slum areas of the cities, which were crammed with badly built houses. Often there were several families living in one room.

There were few sewers or drains. People flung their rubbish and sewage into the river. As there was no running water, they drank water from wells or from the river. This meant that diseases caught from dirty water swept the cities regularly. The most common were typhoid, cholera and dysentery, which killed thousands of people, both rich and poor. Although some rich people had the luxury of water piped to their homes, the water still came from the river. Prince Albert, Queen Victoria's husband, died of typhoid.

COUNTRY LIFE

"I started work scaring birds when I was six or seven years old. I worked all the time it was light, up to 12 hours in the summer. If I fell asleep, the farmer would whip me as punishment," a farm worker said, remembering his boyhood in the 1860s.

Most people who lived in the country worked for farmers whose farms were part of a big estate owned by a rich gentleman. Farm workers' children started work as soon as they were old enough to pick up stones or scare birds off the crops. Older boys did the heavy work on the farm, like ploughing and harvesting. Girls helped in the house and dairy and looked after the animals.

The children of the estate owner seldom saw the village children, unless they became servants on the estate. The boys of the family were away at school for most of the year; the girls were looked after by a governess, who would make sure they did not play, or get too friendly with, the servants.

▷ **Working boys were put in charge of the farm horses** from the age of 10.

△ **A rich mother and daughter visit a sick family.** The poor could not afford to buy fruit (so had few vitamins) or to pay a doctor when someone was sick.

◁ **A family photographed in the country in 1860.** This family was not rich enough to own an estate, but it had a house in the town and another house in the country.

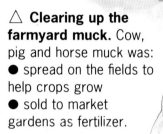

△ **Clearing up the farmyard muck.** Cow, pig and horse muck was:
● spread on the fields to help crops grow
● sold to market gardens as fertilizer.

◁ **Village children in** clothes outgrown by older ones. Often boys had to wear their older sister's clothes.

△ **The eldest daughter** of this country family is leaving home to 'go into service', working as a live-in servant.

▽ **A rattle for scaring crows away from the crops.** The youngest children did this job.

Poor children's homes were small, draughty and cramped, built from local stone, or the cheapest building materials. Their families were often large. The whole family had to work very hard on the farm, all through the year. The children had very little time to play or to go to school. They ate mostly bread and vegetables. They could not afford to buy meat, but ate wild animals, like rabbits, illegally trapped in the fields. If they were lucky, their parents could afford to keep a cow or some chickens. Then they had eggs to eat and milk to drink as well.

MINES AND FACTORIES

"My girls work in the factory. When they get home they fall asleep with supper still in their mouths," a woman in Manchester told a visitor to the mill in 1842. Life was bad in the mines too. A boy said: "We worked the traps that kept the air moving round the mine. The managers beat us to keep us awake."

▽ **Older children working in a Yorkshire fabric mill.** Not until the 1870s were laws passed to stop young children working in factories, mills and mines.

The government sent people to inspect the mines and factories. They found that many of the workers were women and children, because they could be paid less than men. Often the children were the only members of a family who could get work in factory towns. They worked long hours in appalling conditions. Factories were dirty and noisy. The machines were dangerous, and no safety precautions were taken. Children working in the cotton mills had to crawl into spinning machines to tie broken threads on the bobbins. The machines were not turned off while they did this.

▷ **A family making wire brushes at home.** Many families worked at badly paid jobs at home. They made ordinary things like brushes, paper streamers, and match-boxes like those above.

Laws were passed all through the period to raise the age at which children could start work in mines and factories, to limit their working hours, and make sure they had proper rest breaks. But things only got better if the factory or mine owners decided to obey the law. Often they did not do so. Poor parents often did not want factory owners to obey the law – they needed their children to start work as young as possible. They needed the money to live. Even with the children earning, families could only just afford to buy bread, potatoes and sometimes cheese to eat. Even secondhand clothes and shoes were too expensive for them.

▷ **A girl selling matches.**

▽ **Underground in a coal mine.** In this picture there is plenty of space to move, with tracks laid for the wagons. In other places the miners had to squeeze through narrow tunnels.

▽ **Shifts changing at a coal mine.**
● Ponies are used to move the coal wagons. In the early 1800s, the coal was hauled by women and children.
● The wagons run on rails. In some mines, ponies were replaced by steam engines, which were the earliest version of steam trains.

LIVING IN TOWNS

An average Victorian family had six children; Queen Victoria had nine. Feeding, clothing and cleaning up after everyone was a lot of work and it was hard to keep the household running smoothly. Anyone who could afford it had servants to do some of the work.

△ **A coal scuttle from the living room of the home of a rich family.**

Rich families had an army of servants, each with their own particular job in the house, garden or coach house. Boys and girls started working 'in service' from as young as ten. The girls started as scullery maids, peeling vegetables and washing up. Boys started as 'boots' (there were a lot of boots to clean!). Boys could also work in the gardens or as stable boys to help the coachman.

Middle-class families had fewer servants. But they might still have a butler, nanny, cook, and several maids, as well as a coachman and gardeners with at least a boy to help each of them.

Poor children did not always work as servants. Boys worked in shops, as delivery boys. Girls were less able to find shop work, unless it was out of sight of the customers.

▽ **A maid from a well-off household.** The way she is dressed shows that she was not a kitchen maid but a 'lady's maid', who waited on the lady of the house.

△ **Victorian doll's houses were often furnished just like a real home.** This one shows how the furniture in the kitchen was plain and simple, but in the rest of the house it was much more decorative.

▷ **A worker's house from about 1880.** In the illustration, parts of the house have been cut away to see inside the rooms. Meals are cooked and eaten in the living room (left), and the washing up done in the scullery (centre). Upstairs, in the back bedroom, lives a lodger. Alongside the house is an outside toilet and a coal shed. In the yard, the father is collecting coal for the fires and the mother and daughter are putting washed clothes on a line to dry in the air.

Most remaining Victorian houses have been modernized and now have bathrooms, indoor toilets, electricity and running water.

▽ **Washday and household jobs in a working-class home.** Many terraced homes like these are still lived in today.

Even better-off working-class families had help if they could afford it. Often they paid the daughter of a neighbour to come in each day. The worst job was as a live-in 'maid of all work', the only servant in the home. One girl who did this job said, "I thought it would be better than being a scullery maid. But I had to do all the work and there was no-one to talk to while I was working. I cried myself to sleep each night and moved back to a bigger house as soon as I could, for the company."

◁ **Poor children were often glad to go into service** away from their cramped homes and overcrowded streets (shown in the photograph above of 1889). In the illustration, a girl servant is washing clothes in the scullery.

THE BOTTOM OF THE HEAP

"There are thousands of neglected children in our city, prowling the streets begging or stealing their daily bread," wrote journalist Henry Mayhew in 1862. "Some have no parents, others are sent by parents to beg and steal. Many must live by thieving."

Children working in mines, factories and on farms had a hard life. But there were some children, especially in London, who had an even harder life. These were children living on the very edge of starvation. They were forced to beg or steal to live. Or they had to fish for wood, coal and other things out of the disease-ridden mud of the River Thames, to sell for a few pennies. Many of them died before reaching adulthood.

△ **A boy chimney sweep.** His work was dirty, dangerous, but well paid. Cleaning shoes and sweeping the streets were some of the better-paid street jobs.

◁ **The police discover a group of homeless children sleeping out on the rooftops of London.** There were many children like this there because:
● they were orphans
● they had run away from cruel parents
● they had run away from cruel masters.
Thomas Barnado (left), a doctor, took a special interest in these homeless children. In 1867 he started to set up a series of homes for orphans to live in. There are still many family care centres named after him today.

△ **Some people, not always the poor, emigrated**, hoping for a better life in another country. This Victorian painting is called *The Last of England*.

△ **Tramps being moved on by the police in St James's Park, London.** Some people moved around the country looking for work, with some success.

The very poorest families could not pay rent for a house and were homeless. They could either sleep on the streets and beg a living, or they could go to the workhouse. Workhouses were set up by the government to provide people who had no work, no money and no homes with a place to sleep, food and work. But there was a price to pay. Families were split up on arrival; the workhouses were divided into male and female areas. The clothes were uncomfortable and seldom fitted, and the beds were in huge, bare dormitories. The food was tasteless and there was not much of it. The work was hard. Many families preferred to live on the streets.

Children whose parents died, or who ran away from home, were put into orphanages by relatives who did not want them, by people who found them wandering, or by the police. Conditions were similar to those in workhouses. Orphans were hired out to do dirty jobs, like sweeping chimneys.

△ **People waiting to be admitted to a workhouse.** Inside the workhouse (shown right) the women were separated from their husbands and children. They were given workhouse clothes and sent to the womens' 'ward' where they slept, ate and worked.

CHRISTMAS AND RELIGION

**"I must not play on Sunday, because it is a sin.
Tomorrow will be Monday, and then I can begin."
This rhyme sums up many Victorian children's
Sundays – they had to wear their best clothes, go to
church at least once in the day, and be even quieter
and better behaved than usual.**

Sundays for children of the rich and
middle class were very dull. They were
allowed books and toys, but only if the
books told religious or 'moral' tales, and
only if the toys had a religious theme.
But while religion made Sundays dull, it
also provided some very special days.
The most important of these, to a child,
was Christmas. Many of our Christmas
traditions were introduced in the
Victorian period. They include the
sending of Christmas cards, which
was made popular by the new
'Penny Post' mail service.

▷ **Presents, like this
Noah's Ark and
animals (above), were
opened on Christmas
Eve.** This meant that
Christmas Day itself
could be more like a
normal Sunday.

▷ **A family celebrate
Christmas Eve at
home.** Among the
Christmas traditions
introduced or revived at
this time were:
● a Christmas fir tree –
this was a German
tradition. Victoria's
husband, Albert, was
German, and he is said
to have begun the
tradition in this country.
● evergreen wreaths
● holly, mistletoe and
ivy as decorations
● candles and other
decorations for the tree
● Christmas cards
● carol singing.

▷ **Children queuing for breakfast from the Salvation Army.** These breakfasts cost a farthing (a quarter of an old penny) each and were often the only hot meal the children had all day.

▽ **Two young girls take their Christmas presents** from stockings placed at the end of their bedstead.

◁ **Selling Christmas carol sheets** outside a church. Christmas cards were first sold in 1843, the same year that Charles Dickens wrote his story, *A Christmas Carol*.

▽ **Children were expected to say their prayers every night before going to bed.**

Poor children had a very different experience of Sunday, and of religion in general. The only experience most poor children had of religion was the work of church organizations and charities like the Salvation Army, who organized shelter and food for the very poor, and sometimes country outings for the children. Churches also organized schools for workers' children, including 'ragged schools' for the very poorest.

There were many more deaths from illness in Victorian families than there are today, especially among babies and children. Some of the rituals for mourning these deaths, like photographs of the children laid out after death, may seem morbid now, but they helped people to cope with their grief.

THE VICTORIAN SCHOOL

At the beginning of the Victorian period only rich children could be sure of getting an education. One of the biggest changes in the lives of children was the introduction of government-run schools which all children had to attend.

▽ A 'ragged school' for the poor of Edinburgh, photographed in the 1850s.

△ **A dance class** at Robert Owen's mill school.

In 1837 all education had to be paid for. Rich boys were sent away to school. Rich girls were mostly taught at home. There were a lot of private schools for either girls or boys (no school took both) to which the middle class could send their children. Some of these provided a good education. Others were miserable places, where the children were given little education and even less care. Charles Dickens wrote about a school like this, Dotheboys Hall, in his book *Nicholas Nickleby*.

Most poor children were not educated. They worked instead. But there were a few employers who provided education as well as work for the poor. One of these was Robert Owen, whose school at New Lanark Mill was part of a workers' village.

▽ **Children in Victorian schools sat at desks in rows to work.** They all did the same work at the same time. They recited their lessons out loud or wrote things down using:
● A slate to write on. These slates were like those used to make roofs for houses. Anything that was written on them – in white chalk – could be wiped off, so they could be used over and over.
● Books, pen and ink.

▽ **State-run schools of the 1890s**, like this one and Rugby Boys' Private School (right), were expected to teach formal lessons and to 'toughen the boys up' by rough games and discipline.

Other education for workers' children had to be paid for. Young children went to 'dame schools' often run by local women in their own homes. Then they moved on to the local village school. These schools were run by local groups. The government did not provide education. The first national schools were set up by the churches, although the government did give money to help them open more schools. In 1870 the government set up state schools, but it was not until 1891 that a law was passed to provide compulsory, free, education for all children.

◁ **A tutor teaching rich girls geography** in about 1850. Rich and middle-class girls often had a tutor or, more usually, a governess to teach them to read, write and do sums. Governesses also taught sewing, singing, dancing and languages.

17

PLAY AND GAMES

"I was in hospital with some children much poorer than me. I had never heard of any of the games they talked about. They were all used to playing outside, with other children. We had more toys, but had to play in, on our own. We had less fun."

A doctor's daughter said this, talking about her childhood in the 1890s. Rich and middle-class children had much easier lives than poor children, but they had less freedom to play where they liked and to choose who they played with. Their lives were very carefully managed by adults.

On the other hand, their nurseries or schoolrooms were full of beautiful toys. Boys and girls had different kinds of toys, although some toys, like rocking horses, alphabet cubes, playing cards or board games, were seen as suitable for either. Girls were given dolls and doll's houses, tea sets and sewing kits. Boys were given balls and drums, boats and bricks, marbles and toy trains and whole regiments of toy soldiers.

▷ **Children's books were expensive.** Even rich children would only have owned a few books.

▷ **Children window shopping at a toyshop in London.** Victorians were very fond of mechanical and 'scientific' toys, like the clockwork carriage (left) and the zoetrope (next to the Noah's Ark), which used light to create a flickering, moving-picture show.

Poor children had home-made toys, often made from broken everyday objects. So fishermens' children had wooden dolls made out of broken oars. Mill workers' children had toys made from broken thread-winding bobbins. Lucky children were bought a toy from a penny stall. These cheap toys were made from tin or wood.

Cramped homes meant that most poor children played outside as much as they could. Country children could play in the fields and woods and could fish and swim in rivers or ponds. Town children played in the streets, with different games through the year, often ending up with 'larks' like knocking on windows.

Special books and magazines were produced as suitable Sunday reading. The stories in these books would be re-tellings of Bible stories, or stories where there was a Christian message about good behaviour.

◁ **Poor children spent a lot of time playing in the street.** They played games with stones and other bits of rubbish. Boys played marbles and girls played hopscotch and skipping games (if they could find a bit of rope or clothesline). Sometimes a street organist, like this one, came by. Children could dance to the music, or just watch the antics of the monkeys that collected the money after a performance.

◁ **Lead soldiers were a very popular toy for boys.** Britain had a large empire, and a large army to defend it.

HOLIDAYS AND ENTERTAINMENT

In Middlesbrough a local lady remarked, "the two music halls in the town are always full. The cheapest places are the front of the gallery or the pit, where boys of six or seven eagerly pay a penny to watch the show. Boys and men and women go."

Music halls were a working-class amusement. Rich people went to the opera or the theatre. These were not really for children's entertainment, although theatres might put on a pantomime at Christmas. Working-class boys went to the music hall. Their sisters did not – they were at home, working. Rich children usually spent holidays on the family country estate, although their parents might go abroad to France or Switzerland. They might be allowed to go as they got older. Middle-class children were sometimes taken away for a week or two at the seaside.

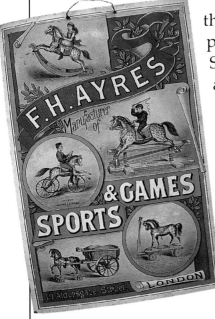

▷ **A visit to the circus.** There were various occasional treats like circus visits:
● **Fairs** were mostly held once a year. Some had one or two rides, and barrows selling treats like 'hokey pokey' (ice cream).
● Poorer children watched entertainments set up in the street. The Punch and Judy man was the most common.

◁ **Books explaining the rules of sports and games.** Many children spent school holidays playing games, with only the occasional trip.

▷ **Children could make their own entertainments** with toys like this.

▽ **Families at work, harvesting the hops in Kent** – in about 1880.

△ **Ramsgate Sands, painted in 1856.** A day by the seaside was a popular treat. Even in hot weather, people did not undress and sunbathe – it was not considered proper.

Growth of the railways from the 1850s onwards made a big difference to holidays for the poor. The railways could take workers from London and the factory towns to the countryside. There were special cheap day 'excursion' trains, which meant that working-class people could afford to go to the seaside for the day.

Women and children could also spend a week or two fruit or hop picking. Hundreds of people from the East End of London set off to the hop fields of Kent each year to pick the hops that would be made into beer. They were usually given a barn full of straw to sleep in, and were paid just enough to be able to feed themselves for the stay. Children were sometimes given picnics or trips by charities or church groups.

An Era of Changes

Joseph Terry wrote an account of his life in 1865. He said of his childhood, "When I was a lad I had to go to work every day from the age of six. Now this business is nearly all done by machine, and poor children are either at school or better employed, for higher wages."

Between 1837 and 1901 a lot of things changed for children, especially for those from poor families. More care was taken over things that affected their health, like sanitation. Laws were passed to make sure that they did not start work so young, that they worked reasonable hours, and that they went to school.

Things changed for the children of the middle classes too. New inventions (such as the telephone and the typewriter) had created new jobs for these children to aim at. This was especially true for girls who, rather than having to marry, could try to earn their living.

Life for rich children, on the other hand, changed much less. They were still brought up by servants and saw little of their parents. Boys went away to school, girls were brought up to marry rich men.

▽ **A child patient** in Great Ormond Street Hospital for Sick Children in London in 1867. By 1901 poor children were given free hospital care.

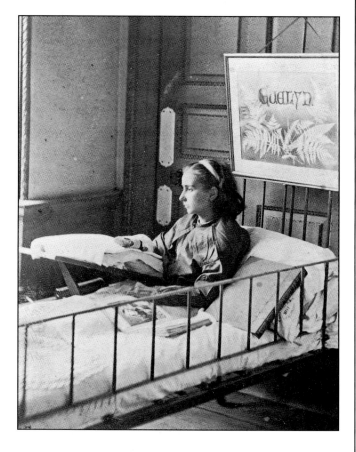

▷ **Charity workers**, like these Salvation Army midwives, did more to help the poor.

◁ **The Houses of Parliament and Big Ben clock tower** in London, built in the 1840s and 1850s, are fine examples of Victorian architecture.

GLOSSARY

bobbins wooden cylinders, about 30 cm long. Thread was wound round them, then this was woven through other fixed threads to make cloth.

'boots' a boy whose only job in a big house was to clean the boots and shoes.

British Empire lands that Britain controlled all over the world.

dairy place in the farm where milk was stored. Here the cream was taken off and cheese was made from milk.

dormitories large rooms where lots of people sleep in beds set in rows.

emigration going to live in a different country from the one you were born in.

estates large areas of land, with farms and villages on them, all owned by one person.

factory where lots of people work, making one thing (like cloth), using machines to do some of the work.

midwives nurses who look after women while they are pregnant and when their babies are very young.

mill here, a factory which makes cloth.

national all over the country or nation.

orphan a child whose parents are both dead.

Penny Post the postal system, introduced in 1840, when it cost just one penny to send a letter.

private schools parents paid to send their children to these schools. Often children had to live there during term time.

scullery a room near the kitchen, with a sink for washing up.

slum part of a town with very badly built and overcrowded houses where the poorest people lived.

traps wooden doors which were opened and closed to allow fresh air into the mine.

Victorian Britain

This map shows the position of the major locations mentioned in this book.

Places mentioned in the text

Kingussie

New Lanark · Whitburn
· Edinburgh
Rothbury·

Cookstown·
Dungannon·

Barnard
Castle · York
Blackpool· Manchester
· Salford Styal
Beaumaris Knutsford
Stafford· ·Derby
Leominster ·Rugby

High Royston
Neath Wycombe
Cardiff· ·London
Bath Reading ·Ramsgate
Tiverton ·East
Brighton Grinstead
Tintagel·

INDEX